SOUL POWER

AN AGENDA FOR A CONSCIOUS HUMANITY

by Anne Baring and Scilla Elworthy

Design by Tania Coke

A CIP catalog record for this book is available from the Library of Congress.

ISBN: 1-4392-3415-9

EAN: 9781439234150

With grateful thanks to NASA and the Hubble Heritage Team for the images of deep space, used on the cover pages and throughout this book.

No problem can be solved from the consciousness that created it...

AS THE ECONOMIC AND SOCIAL STRUCTURES OF OUR WORLD COLLAPSE AROUND US, WEBSITES AROUND THE WORLD ARE QUOTING EINSTEIN'S FAMOUS WORDS.

WELL AND GOOD, BUT HOW DO WE MOVE TO A NEW LEVEL OF CONSCIOUSNESS?

First, we understand that the crisis of our times is not only an ecological, political and financial crisis but a spiritual one. The answers we seek will not come from the limited consciousness that now rules the world. They can only grow from a deeper understanding born of the union of heart and head.

This union would enable us to see that all life is one, that each one of us participates in a cosmic life of immeasurable dimensions.

Our health and the health of the planet require this deeper insight, this sense of belonging to a greater whole. It alone can help us to recover values that have been increasingly lost until we now live without them—and without even noticing they have gone.

Second, we need to be aware of the powerful influence on our culture of two deeply held beliefs that have long governed our actions. Each of these beliefs, presented as incontrovertible truth, has distorted our view of reality and has led to our alienation from nature and from soul:

a) The belief that 'God' is separate from this world and that we were given dominion over the Earth. Western civilisation has developed on the foundation of a fundamental split between spirit and nature, creator and creation.

b) The secular belief of scientific materialism, which might be summarised as follows:

- The universe came into being by chance
- Matter is primary and gives rise to mind as a secondary phenomenon
- Our consciousness is a by-product of the neurology and biochemistry of the brain. Our ability to think, feel and imagine is no more than the product of our brain cells
- The death of the physical brain is the end of consciousness
- 'God' is an unnecessary hypothesis and the concept of soul or spirit is an erroneous fiction
- We can impose our will on nature to serve our needs
- There is no transcendent purpose or meaning to our lives other than the fulfilment of those needs.

Third, we could move beyond the constriction of these beliefs towards an alternative worldview which could reconnect us with nature and with soul, so restoring our fragmented being to wholeness, namely:

- There is an invisible or transcendent order of reality out of which the phenomenal world arises
- The universe is conscious and there are many dimensions to it
- Our human consciousness is integral to that greater consciousness, even though it is still partially developed or immature
- Consciousness in some form survives the death of the physical body
- What we have called spirit is continually creating life in the universe, our planet and ourselves. All is one life, one energy. We as humans participate in this energy
- The soul is not confined to the life of the individual: it is a vast web of relationships connecting invisible fields of energy – moving at faster rates of vibration – with the denser field of physical reality
- The purpose of our lives on this planet is to live in growing communion with this web of relationships.

One story is that of a dead universe that assumes matter is the sole reality and consciousness but an illusion. This is the standard story of contemporary Western science. The other is the story of a living universe that takes consciousness to be the primary reality. This is a new story emerging as a synthesis of ancient religious wisdom and the data of the scientific leading edge – and it potentially changes everything.

David Korten, *Mind Before Matter* [1]

Only those who will risk going too far can possibly find out how far one can go.

T S Eliot

THE SHIFT

The shift from seeing ourselves as separate to seeing ourselves as participants in an unceasing miracle of creation, is not just a shift from one set of values to another. It transforms the human story. After fourteen billion years of evolution, we become responsible for more than just our patch.

We become capable of deeper reflection.

We get a longer term perspective.

We grow up.

A human being is part of the whole called by us universe, a part limited in time and space. He experiences himself, his thoughts and feelings as something separated from the rest, a kind of optical delusion of his consciousness. This delusion is a kind of prison for us, restricting us to our personal desires and to affection for a few persons nearest to us. Our task must be to free ourselves from this prison by widening our circle of compassion to embrace all living creatures and the whole of nature in its beauty.

Albert Einstein

THE SLEEPING BEAUTY

A living relationship with the soul is the treasure that we have lost. It is not by chance that the story of the Sleeping Beauty has survived over the centuries in different forms in most cultures, because it describes a profound truth about humanity. The soul lies spellbound in the enchanted castle of our inner life, waiting to be redeemed from its millennia-long trance by the longing for greater understanding of our predicament – the longing that alone can penetrate the hedge of thorns that guards and conceals it.

THE HEDGE OF THORNS

The hedge of thorns is our inheritance of beliefs, whether religious or scientific. It presents the greatest obstacle to the recovery of the lost treasure and vanquishes all but the most persistent.

The fact that we are now on the verge of destroying the Earth and each other is the direct result of living for so many centuries in ignorance of our most profound need – to know that our lives are rooted in the life of the soul.

Knowledge of the holy unity of life, reverence for nature, trust in the powers of the creative imagination, in the atrophied faculty of intuition – all these are needed to help us recover that lost, instinctive relationship with life. They could open the way through the hedge of thorns. This could be the decisive factor between our survival or destruction as a species.

In the past, the word 'soul' conveyed meaning: the greatest artists, poets and mystics were engaged in keeping people in touch with their soul. Today, however, the word means nothing in a secular culture that is unconscious of the existence and value of an inner life.

For such a culture, the soul is asleep, under a spell, held in bondage to beliefs and habits of behaviour that deny us access to the deeper levels of our being. Our brilliant technological culture inflicts intolerable stress on us because it grants no value to feelings and allows no time for relationship with the soul, no time to awaken to the beauty and wonder of the extraordinary treasure that lies hidden within and all around us.

Somewhere in Chartres Cathedral, these words are inscribed

O Awaken not the Beauty until the time comes.

Myths and fairy tales awaken and nourish the imagination.
The imagination reconnects us with forgotten instincts.
When we are not in touch with our inner life, it is as if a vital
part of us is asleep.
It cannot communicate with us, nor we with it; we cannot live
to the fullest extent of which we are capable.
A civilisation will die when it has lost its connection to soul.
Those who say there is no mystery to understand
literally kill their instinctive life, their soul.

WE LIVE IN A DANGEROUS TIME BECAUSE OUR ENTRENCHED BELIEF SYSTEMS ARE ROOTED IN FEAR.

Germany, 1944/45

We kill at every step, not only in wars, riots, and executions. We kill when we close our eyes to poverty, suffering, and shame. In the same way all disrespect for life, all hard-heartedness, all indifference, all contempt is nothing else than killing. With just a little witty scepticism we can kill a good deal of the future in a young person. Life is waiting everywhere, the future is flowering everywhere, but we only see a small part of it and step on much of it with our feet.

Hermann Hesse [2]

OUR SURVIVAL HABITS OF BEHAVIOUR ENCOURAGE GREED, CRUELTY AND THE DESIRE FOR POWER.

Gaza, 2009

There is no purpose and there is no hope in this war, that is about to swallow us by the flames of bereavement; there is no purpose to the mutual annihilation and to the approaching silence of death afterwards.

Families of Bereaved Palestinians [3]

ARE WE TO BE THE CAUSE OF THE SIXTH GREAT EXTINCTION OF LIFE ON THIS PLANET ?

If we could see ourselves through the eyes of another planet, the effects of our behaviour would be clearly apparent:

- The exploitation of the resources of the Earth for our own use
- The pollution of earth, sea and air with our toxic waste
- The wanton cruelty to animals
- The clearing of the great rain forests in order to grow crops that will supply fuel for our industrial expansion and cattle for our food
- The contamination of food and water with toxins and pesticides
- The development of weapons of mass destruction that could destroy the beauty and life of the earth
- The murder of men, women and children in war
- The destruction of the miracle of our bodies through the use of targeted explosives
- The mute agony of orphaned, abandoned and maimed children
- The greed which drives us to consume incessantly while others starve
- The desolation, deprivation and violence of city slums worldwide.

War devastates not only our physical being but our very soul—for the entire culture as well as for the individual. In war, chaos overwhelms compassion, violence replaces cooperation, instinct replaces rationality, gut dominates mind. When drenched in these conditions, the soul is disfigured and can become lost for life.

Edward Tick, *War and the Soul* [4]

The current impact of mankind on the bio-diversity of the planet can be compared to the impact of a ten mile wide meteor on earth 65 million years ago.

David Attenborough [5]

WHAT INERADICABLE SCARS DO WE INFLICT ON OUR CHILDREN?

WHY ARE WE STILL LOCKED INTO THIS HABIT OF WAR?

All nature seemed filled with peace-giving power and beauty.

Is there not room enough for men to live in peace in this magnificent world, under this infinite starry sky? How is it that wrath, vengeance, or the lust to kill their fellow men can persist in the soul of man in the midst of this entrancing Nature? Everything evil in the heart of man ought, one would think, to vanish in contact with Nature, in which beauty and goodness find their most direct expression.

War? What an incomprehensible phenomenon! When reason asks itself, is it just? Is it necessary?, an internal voice always answers no. Only the permanence of this unnatural phenomenon makes it natural, and only the instinct for self preservation makes it just.

Tolstoy, *The Raid: A Volunteer's Story* [6]

Man, the child of Mother Earth, would not be able to survive the crime of matricide if he were to commit it. The penalty for this would be self-annihilation.

Arnold Toynbee, *Mankind and Mother Earth* [7]

We are living now in a time of stupendous scientific discoveries that are enlarging our vision of the universe, shattering old concepts about the nature of reality. Yet the delicate organism of life on our planet and the survival of our species are threatened as never before by the drive for dominance and control of nature. This brutal desire to conquer and master nature for our own purposes shows no respect for the Earth. It disregards the mortal danger of our interference with the fragile web of relationships upon which life on this planet depends. We are an integral part of this great web of life, formed over countless millions of years. We will not survive unless we respect it.

It is as if this mortal danger is forcing us to take a great leap in our evolution that we might never have made, were we not driven to it by the crisis facing us. Because our capacity for destruction, both military and environmental, is so much greater today than it was fifty years ago, and will be still greater tomorrow, we have perhaps only a few decades in which to heal ourselves and the planet.

In relation to the earth, we have been autistic for centuries. Only now have we begun to listen with some attention and with a willingness to respond to the earth's demands that we cease our industrial assault, that we abandon our inner rage against the conditions of our earthly existence, that we renew our human participation in the grand liturgy of the universe.

Thomas Berry, *The Dream of the Earth* [8]

My view of our planet was a glimpse of divinity.
Edgar Mitchell, Astronaut

THE TIME IS NOW

Now is a pivotal time. There is an immense opportunity to involve the whole of humanity in an evolutionary advance, if only we can understand what is happening and why.

So :

- How do we recover our lost sense of being part of something totally sacred?
- How do we develop respect and compassion for the life of the Earth in all its forms?
- How do we find ways of meeting the deepest needs of the human heart for love, relatedness and connection?
- How can we recognise – in our daily lives – that beauty is intrinsic to cosmic order and that harmony is the foundation of nature and the human soul?

Only after the last tree has been cut down,
Only after the last river has been poisoned,
Only after the last fish has been caught,
Only then will you find that money cannot be eaten.

Cree Indian Prophecy

When a caterpillar first begins this transformation, an entirely new kind of cell begins to appear inside the caterpillar that scientists call Imaginal cells. These cells contain the imagining or blueprint of a whole new being.

At first as these cells appear, they are attacked and resisted by the caterpillar, but gradually as more of these appear, they grow stronger and begin to cluster together to form the first organs of the new creature. Eventually clusters of cells will form extensions of connective tissue that bridge these small groups of cells into a larger form. The old form literally dies, as a new being is born from within the old.

This is what is happening to humanity. Every person who carries universal peace in their hearts represents an Imaginal cell. In every nation there are groups of these cells that have begun to cluster together in specific regions to form an organ of peace, and gradually these groups are weaving a web of peace throughout the land.

Michael White,
An Imaginal Journey of Peace [9]

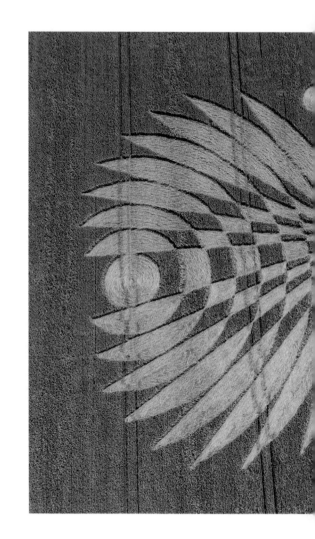

No longer need we see man as an insignificant spare part in a mindless mechanism, but rather the cosmos and the human akin because informed with the one life, in which the inner universe finds perpetually its correspondence in the outer world, a natural world which is an expression of the one mind that moves through all things, from stone and star to plants, animals, flowers, which are all, as we are ourselves, living expressions of that living mind.

Kathleen Raine,
The Underlying Order and Other Essays [10]

RE-BALANCING HEAD AND HEART: INTEGRATING THE MASCULINE AND FEMININE DIMENSIONS OF OUR BEING

Humanity is undergoing a difficult rite of passage, a 'dark night of the soul' prior to the birth of a new consciousness. There is a huge disruption in the social order as old social patterns and old institutions disintegrate.

Some take refuge in fundamentalism – an attempt to perpetuate the control system and the values of the old order – a desperate grasping at certainty and security.

However, for others, this time is a supreme opportunity to respond to an evolutionary awakening of global proportions: the activation of the lost feminine principle of soul. This awakening asks us to open a dialogue with our inner world – to become receptive to the voice of the soul and to listen to our deepest instincts.

If man's relationship to Nature is nothing but that of technological victory, it amounts to a loveless union of Man and Nature, a rape, and this will end in perdition.

Karl Stern, *The Flight from Woman* [11]

Like the magma of the Earth's molten core, the Feminine is pushing up from below the level of our conscious lives, manifesting as a call for radical change in the way we perceive and live life, urging us to reconnect with nature, soul and cosmos.

An epochal shift is taking place in the contemporary psyche, a reconciliation between the two great polarities, a union of opposites: a sacred marriage between the long-dominant but now alienated masculine and the long-suppressed but now ascending feminine...Our time is struggling to bring forth something fundamentally new in human history: We seem to be witnessing, suffering, the birth labour of a new reality, a new form of human existence, a 'child' that would be the fruit of this great archetypal marriage.

Richard Tarnas, *The Passion of the Western Mind* [12]

The influence of the feminine principle is responsible for the growing engagement of women in our culture, in the growth of the environmental movement, in many new approaches to healing both mind and body, in the engagement of hundreds of thousands of people in helping both the planet and the victims of persecution, deprivation and war. Together, these different channels of influence are inviting new perspectives on life, new ways of living that bring together body, soul, mind and spirit. They draw all of us to work together towards the goal of rescuing this planet and the lives of future generations from our unconscious habits of behaviour.

When feminine and masculine principles are out of balance there is oppression. Not oppression just of the feminine, but oppression of the masculine as well because you cannot oppress one without distorting both. Oppression does not discriminate. It oppresses all. Its invisible and pervasive force constricts the heart, suppresses the spirit and censors expression. When the focus of our attention lives in stillness and animates balance and renewal, there is an endless breadth of possibilities that nourish heart, spirit and creativity.

Rose von Thater-Braan, *Mind Before Matter* [13]

Over the last few millennia, the feeling of belonging to the life of an invisible entity beyond the community of tribe or nation, something experienced as numinous, immeasurable and all-embracing, was gradually lost and with it the sense of participation in a sacred, living universe – a vast web of life where every single creature and element of life was connected to every other.

Our own consciousness, which includes the whole spectrum of experience between instinct and the rational intellect as well as the furthest reaches of the imagination, could participate once again in this greater planetary and cosmic soul of which our culture has lost all awareness.

Our actual identity or experience of who we are is vastly bigger than we thought – we are moving from a strictly personal consciousness to a conscious appreciation of ourselves as integral to the cosmos. In this new paradigm, our sense of identity takes on a paradoxical and mysterious quality: We are both observer and observed, knower and that which is known. We are each completely unique yet completely connected with the entire universe. Awakening to the miraculous nature of our identity as simultaneously unique and interconnected with a living universe can help us overcome the species-arrogance and sense of separation that threaten our future.

Duane Elgin, *Mind Before Matter* [14]

The life we know is an excitation on the surface
of an immeasurable sea of cosmic energy
that is continually surging, dancing, flowing into being.
In every galaxy, every star, every planet, every cell of our being
the universe is bursting into existence from this womb or sea of being.
What does this mean for us?
It means that when we are in touch with this incredible idea,
each one of us becomes co-creator with that mysterious process,
at one with our starry source.

A deeper understanding, born of the union of heart and head, would awaken us to the sacredness, oneness and divinity of life.

We would begin to heal the deep wounds inflicted by our unconscious habits of behaviour.

The meaning and purpose of life is to be discovered neither through faith nor through accumulating knowledge about the known world, but through inward transformation and the development of the eye of the heart.

Opening the Eye of the Heart requires practice,
patience and trust to bring it into being.
When we are prepared to become but a humble servant of life,
devoted to caring for it and healing it,
we become free from all fear.
We are then able to resonate with life,
harmoniously and ecstatically.

So, what changes would such an understanding bring about?

A change of understanding in one person activates change in others: a new way of responding to one issue, such as the pathology of war, the dangers of globalisation, or new methods of healing, accelerates change. Like leaven in bread, the awakening of a few individuals is raising the whole loaf. A door is opening that previously was closed; a new way of living is becoming accessible to many. Thousands of people are crowding through this door, drawn by a unified image of life. A vast new panorama is opening to our vision, and it includes the following insights:

- All aspects of life are interconnected and interdependent
- We have a responsibility to act in defence of nature; and this responsibility requires a global strategy for radical change
- The changes now needed are not coming from governments, but from the pressure on governments of people demanding and implementing change from below
- Our values need to be grounded in responsibility towards planetary life
- There is a compelling need for a humility that is consistent with our limited view as humans.

These insights are moving us towards a more mature spirituality that includes environmental awareness and a more ethical technology that would not injure the planet. It could even help to undo the harm already done.

This understanding is reflected and embodied in our society, where new discoveries and initiatives are pouring into the culture from every direction. Here are just a few:

- The ability to communicate face to face over vast distances
- The ability to activate networks of like-minded people across the planet
- The ability to influence government policies by means of world-wide internet pressure
- The recognition that we have incredible powers to heal ourselves and our world
- The fact that meditation, visualisation and prayer can effect remarkable changes in the neuro-chemistry of the body and affect others at a distance.

I am done with great things and big plans, great institutions and big success. I am for those tiny, invisible, loving, human forces that work from individual to individual, creeping through the crannies of the world like so many rootlets, or like the capillary oozing of water, which, if given time, will rend the hardest monuments of pride.

William James, *The Will to Believe* [15]

What would a world be like based on a mindset that understood that all is One and interconnected?

How soon could the knowledge that we live in a participatory world initiate change in our thinking about war, and our desecration of the planet?

Would a world aware of the primacy of consciousness be akin to the world as seen by some of the indigenous peoples?

Would we then see the cosmos as a living presence; and the whole universe, and all of nature, as intelligent?...

Would we discover that the physical laws of the universe were 'habits', evolving rather than immutable?

Would we begin to sense other realities and other dimensions?

When we realized that time and space are not fundamental dimensions underlying reality, would it change forever our ideas about death?

Would we strive for unconditional love?

How would human relationships, social justice, poverty, science, medicine, politics, the government, and the military be reframed according to consciousness-primary perspectives?

Trish Pfeiffer, Prologue to Mind Before Matter [16]

SUPPOSE WE DARED

Suppose we dared to tell our children from earliest childhood about the Web of Life, describing it as something that they belong to, participate in, so that they could attune their awareness to it, could learn how to listen to it, converse with it and develop a deepening relationship with it. Suppose parents and teachers told children that each one of them has a special gift, and that they can learn how to nourish and express that gift to the best of their ability. Suppose they told them that education is about learning how to develop wisdom and insight, in order to enjoy making a living. And that each one is unique and beloved, with the possibility of equal access to the source.

If we came to believe that the universe was not composed of 'dead matter' but living, intelligent, self-emergent energy-matter, if we came to believe that inside the creative pulse of evolution was not simply blind luck and patient sifting but ingenuity and even forethought, this might be a universe that we would want to enter into communion with. If we felt that our individual creativity had a counterpart, a silent partner, hidden in the surrounding Meta-universe, this might be a partnership we would seek to deepen. If we felt that the love we feel for our children were mirrored in a love the universe feels for her child, this might be an embrace that we would seek to cultivate.

Christopher Bache, *Mind Before Matter* [17]

THE GREAT WORK

Acting together under the inspiration of a new vision of our responsibility to this planet, we may be able to transform the deficient values that now drive our governments. This is the Great Work that is now in progress as more and more people awaken to the values that express our responsibility towards life, each other and the planet as a whole.

Inspiration is not garnered from litanies of what is flawed; it resides in humanity's willingness to restore, redress, reform, recover, re-imagine, and reconsider. Healing the wounds of the Earth and its people does not require saintliness or a political party. It is not a liberal or conservative activity. It is a sacred act.

Paul Hawken, *Blessed Unrest* [18]

We have the opportunity to join together to experience what very few generations in history have had the privilege of knowing: a generation mission, a compelling moral purpose, a shared and unifying cause, and an opportunity to work together to choose a future for which our children will thank us instead of cursing our failure to protect them against a clear and present danger with equally clear and devastating future consequences.

Al Gore [19]

FORMULATING THE NEW VALUES

As the wisdom embodied in the new values grows and begins to outweigh the vested interests of corporations and their influence on governments, we are developing a new ethical and moral framework within which to assess our actions and create an agenda for change. We can expect the following to happen:

- The public refuses to finance the invention, manufacture and sale of weapons that inflict calamitous suffering on human beings and contaminate the soil for millions of years
- As people discover their security within themselves and their communities the need for the security of a nation-state diminishes
- As like-minded people connect to a greater and greater extent across the planet, the willingness of states to fight each other is undermined
- As people become more aware of the interconnection of everything, they reject technologies which harm and pollute the fabric of life, and focus on developing technologies that protect and cherish life.

In a dead universe, consumerism makes sense; in a living universe, simplicity makes sense. If the universe is unconscious and dead at its foundations, then each of us is the product of blind chance among materialistic forces. It is only fitting that we the living exploit on our own behalf that which is not alive. If the universe is lifeless, it has no larger purpose and meaning and neither does human existence. On the other hand, if the universe is conscious and alive, then we are the product of a deep-design intelligence that infuses the entire cosmos.

Duane Elgin, *Mind Before Matter* [20]

We have the power to change the collective dream

Paulo Coelho

THE NEW POLITICAL AGENDA

- A Universal Declaration of Planetary Rights is implemented, following the example of Ecuador
- Agreements are negotiated for global stewardship of scarce resources in order to ensure equitable distribution
- The dumping of poisonous chemicals and nuclear residues in the Third World is prohibited by international law
- A global fund is created to ensure the preservation of the rain forests
- The appropriation of land to grow biofuels is prohibited by international agreement
- Worldwide competition between governments to conserve energy develops, including public naming and shaming of corporate waste of light and heat
- Toxic pollutants and pesticides in food and water are progressively eliminated
- Nuclear technology is abandoned because of the impossibility of disposing of waste with a half life of tens of thousands of years
- Nuclear research and development budgets are re-directed towards developing benign energy systems
- Consumerism as the driving force of economic growth is recognised as a dangerous illusion
- The exploitation of the Earth's resources for the financial benefit of the few becomes unacceptable, just as slavery did
- In the interests of the survival of our own and other species, global agreements are made to limit the size of our families at replacement level
- Skills of mediation instead of the use of force are used to resolve conflict and prevent killing

- Combined military and civilian peace-keeping forces are used to minimise casualties in conflict areas
- International treaties are negotiated to prohibit the sale of weapons
- The trillions of dollars saved from expenditure on weapons are used to feed, house and educate the world's poor
- The skills and subsidies previously used in the manufacture of weapons are redeployed to socially useful products and exports
- Intermediate technologies which assist small communities in the Third World are developed and expanded
- Terrorism is reduced by addressing on a psychological level the anger, hate and humiliation that drive it. Recognising the causes of political violence weakens the habit of demonising the enemy.

We should expect far more of our leaders than we presently do. Never has the need for genuine leadership been greater, and seldom has it been less evident... If we are to navigate the challenges of the decades ahead, what E.O. Wilson calls 'the bottleneck', we will need leaders of great stature, clarity of mind, spiritual depth, courage, and vision. We need leaders who see patterns that connect us across the divisions of culture, religion, geography, and time. We need leadership that draws us together to resolve conflicts, move quickly from fossil fuels to solar power, reverse global environmental deterioration, and empower us to provide shelter, food, medical care, decent livelihood, and education for everyone. We need leadership that is capable of energizing genuine commitment to old and venerable traditions as well as new visions for a global civilization that preserves and honors local cultures, economies, and knowledge.

Imagine a world in which those who purport to lead us must first make a pilgrimage to ground zero at Hiroshima and publicly pledge 'never again'. Imagine a world in which those who purport to lead us must go to Auschwitz and the Killing Fields and pledge publicly 'never again'. Imagine a world in which leaders must go to Bhopal and say to the victims 'We are truly sorry. This will never happen again, anywhere'. Imagine, too, those pilgrim leaders going to hundreds of places where love, kindness, forgiveness, sacrifice, compassion, wisdom, ecological ingenuity, and foresight have been evident.

Imagine a world in which those who purport to lead us must help identify places around the world degraded by human actions and help initiate their restoration. Some areas might take as long as 1000 years to restore, such as the Aral Sea, the Harrapan region in India, the forests of Lebanon, soil fertility in the Middle East, Chesapeake Bay, and the North Atlantic cod fishery. Imagine a world in which those who intend to lead help lift our sights above the daily crisis to the far horizon of what could be.

David Orr [21]

BUT IT'S NOT JUST ABOUT OUR LEADERS.   IT'S ABOUT US.

WE CAN BE THE CHANGE WE WANT TO SEE IN THE WORLD.   TODAY

We can make shifts in our everyday lives – in the way we do things, in the way we think, in how we are. Instead of seeing the current crises as frightening, we can see the opportunity they offer – an opportunity to replace our moribund de-humanised systems with ways of living that value the planet, ways of living that are richer and much more satisfying.

We can make our **domestic** decisions – decisions about travel, heating, shopping – based on the needs of the planet. We can take our business away from de-humanized organizations to more connected ones, where we can form a relationship with a person, such as local barter systems.

In our **workplace**, we can suggest and support moves away from hierarchical structures to horizontal ones that are personalised, connected and enable individuals to develop and thrive. We can demonstrate to leaders and managers that 'top down' change cannot succeed without 'bottom up' consultation and engagement. We can move away from the sickness of ruthless greed and competition, towards an understanding of our path in life, what we are really here to do.

WE COULD DEVELOP NEW SKILLS AND QUALITIES

We shall need **emotional intelligence** – understanding not simply the point of view but the needs of the 'opponent'[22]. Nonviolent communication is now being learned and used by people all over the world, simply because it works, and works wonders[23]. We can also learn how trust is built by taking a course in conflict mediation or negotiation.

Each of us needs to find our **own unique path**: in fact this may be the most important thing we ever do, to perceive how our particular skills can be most useful in the world. We can spend time with a friend or mentor asking questions like 'What is my calling in life?' 'What do I do with ease that others find difficult?'

Sometimes we may be offered opportunities to grow and become more complete human beings. **Servant leadership** is a powerful way to learn how I – as an ego – can step back, and I as a servant can step forward[24].

An on-going practice of reflection or **self-awareness**[25] could become a daily support. Self knowledge enables us to develop the ability to confront and transform darker emotions. Telling a friend about what we fear, and connecting with our deepest feelings, is a way to regain balance.

Invite people in your **community** to come together to share and implement ideas. Ask them what ideas they find most constructive and inspiring and what issues most concern them.

We as human beings are nourished by a **sense of wonder**. On a clear night, go outside and watch the moon and the stars. Care for your body as a miraculous organism that asks to be loved and valued.

HERE IS THE QUINTESSENCE OF WHAT WE COULD DO TO BRING INTO BEING A NEW KIND OF CONSCIOUSNESS

As the relationship between our surface personality and the eternal ground of life grows stronger, we become more aware of its voice, its presence and its subtle guidance. A deepening relationship with this ground can become the inner fabric and focus of our lives. It is an alchemy that we can weave into being with our attention, developing insight through our longing for understanding and connection.

If this path into the depth of ourselves is gently followed, we no longer live life unconsciously, responding blindly to events as they happen. Through this transformation, so gradual and subtle that it is almost imperceptible, our perception of the world is transformed.

Live life as an opportunity to
transform the nectar of experience
into the honey that can heal the world.

When you meditate, see yourself
as a cell in a limitless honeycomb
of golden light.

Imagine, just imagine, this luminous network of
honeycomb cells connecting people in every part
of the world who are trying to lift humanity out
of the dark place we are in now. Imagine that
through this powerful network of relationships a
new consciousness is coming into being…

It comes down to this.

Thinking we are the most intelligent, the most evolved life form thrown up by a foaming, mechanical universe, we commune only with ourselves and keep the cold world at bay.

But if we were to open to a world in which we recognized the blazing intelligence of the cosmic womb that birthed us and everything we see around us, if we began to glimpse the scale and scope of her project and the depth of love that underwrites it, we would turn and face this mysterious world…

We would build up commerce with it until contact deepened into communion, and communion is a sacramental exchange that transforms both parties.

With this pivot, history would turn.

We would begin to value and cultivate the skills of alignment.

We would begin to recognize the symptoms of misalignment in individuals, in institutions and ideologies.

Christopher Bache, *Mind Before Matter* [26]

LIST OF REFERENCES

1. David Korten, *Mind Before Matter, Visions of a New Science of Consciousness*, O Books, Ropley, Hampshire, 2008, p. 138
2. Hermann Hesse
3. Families of Bereaved Palestinians, Open Democracy Website, 20 January 2009
4. Edward Tick, *War and the Soul*, Quest Books, Wheaton, Ill., 2005
5. David Attenborough, BBC2 State of the Planet, 2000
6. Tolstoy, *The Raid: A Volunteer's Story*, 1852, from Anna Politkovskaya's book, *A Small Corner of Hell, Dispatches from Chechnya*, The University of Chicago Press, 2003
7. Arnold Toynbee, *Mankind and Mother Earth*, OUP, 1976
8. Thomas Berry, *The Dream of the Earth*, Sierra Club Books, San Francisco, 1988
9. Michael White, *An Imaginal Journey of Peace*, 22 May 2007
10. Kathleen Raine, *The Underlying Order and Other Essays*, Temenos Academy, London 2008
11. Karl Stern, *The Flight from Woman*, originally published 1966, p. 269
12. Richard Tarnas, *The Passion of the Western Mind*, Ballantyne Books, New York 1991, Epilogue
13. Rose von Thater-Braan, *Mind Before Matter,* p. 260
14. Duane Elgin, *Mind Before Matter,* p. 77
15. William James, *The Will to Believe and Other Essays in Popular Philosophy.* First published 1897
16. Trish Pfeiffer, *Mind Before Matter,* Prologue
17. Christopher Bache, *Mind Before Matter*, p. 274
18. Paul Hawken, *Blessed Unrest*, Viking, New York, 2007
19. Al Gore, from an article in the Sunday Telegraph, 19/11/06
20. Duane Elgin, *Mind Before Matter,* p. 77-8
21. David Orr, *The Case for the Earth*, Resurgence Magazine issue 219; 01/07/2003
22. Try *Emotional Intelligence* by Daniel Goleman
23. Take a course in Nonviolent Communication. www.nonviolentcommunication.com
24. There are courses and practices to suit every need: meditation, yoga, tai chi, co-counselling etc.
25. www.greenleaf.org
26. Christopher Bache, *Mind Before Matter,* p. 279

LIST OF ILLUSTRATIONS

Front cover: The Ant Nebula, Mz3, NASA, ESA and The Hubble Heritage Team

(page 3) The Horsehead Nebula, IC434, NASA, NOAO, ESA and The Hubble Heritage Team

(page 5) Ladder collage, based on photograph by Aradan-Fotolia.com

(page 7) Man Looking Beyond Known Cosmos, Woodcut, Swiss, sixteenth century

(pages 9 and 10) The Rose Bower (Sleeping Beauty) and The Briar Wood (Hedge of Thorns), from The Legend of the Briar Rose by Sir Edward Burne-Jones (1833-1898) courtesy of The Faringdon Collection, Buscot Park, Oxfordshire

(page 13) Barred Spiral Milky Way, R. Hurt (SSC), JPL-Caltech, NASA

(pages 14 and 15) Images of Germany 1944/5 and Gaza 2009, from an email forwarded by Palintlist

(page 17) Photo of Beirut 1985 – Rex Features/Sipa Press

(page 18) Photo of boy in rubbish dump: EPA/Rungroj Yongrit

(page 19) Photo of Jabalya, Gaza – EPA/Ali Ali

(page 20) Boot and Flower collage

(page 21) Hiroshima

(page 23) 'The Blue Marble': Image of Earth from space, NASA

(page 25) Cree Indian – every effort has been made to trace the copyright owner of this photograph

(page 26-27) Crop Circle of Butterfly Hailey Wood 16/7/2007, photo courtesy of Steve Alexander www.temporarytemples.co.uk. See also www.WhatOnEarthTheMovie.com

(page 29) Crop circle of Yin-Yang Image Stantonbury Hill 7/7/2007, photo courtesy Steve Alexander

(page 33) Crop circle of Milk Hill 12/08/2001, photo courtesy Steve Alexander

(page 34) Crop circle of Swallows, Southfield, Alton Priors, July 2008, photo courtesy Steve Alexander

(page 35) Moonrise, Chinese Landscape, Tushita Artwork Studios

(page 36) Red Supergiant Star V838 Monocerotis, NASA, ESA and H E Bond

(page 39) Sombrero, M104, NASA and The Hubble Heritage Team

(page 41) Globular Cluster, M80, The Hubble Heritage Team

(page 43) Colorfully Diverse Children, by J Bryson

(page 45) Courtesy of Ted Giffords, Peace Direct, www.peacedirect.org

(page 47) 'Cosmos', Painting by Robin Baring

(page 49) PS10 Solar Tower, Andalucia, Spain, by Denis Doyle/Getty Images News

(page 51) Photo of Dalai Lama, courtesy of Clive Arrowsmith, London

(page 52-53) Bee and Chive flower by Richard Chaff, Bumblebee and yellow flower by Valerie Loiseleux

(page 54-55) Honeycomb by Petr Kratochvil, Bees by vnlit

(page 56) Galaxy Cluster, NASA, ESA and M J Jee (Johns Hopkins University)

(page 59) Kauri tree in Waipoua Forest, North of Auckland, New Zealand, courtesy Michael Baigent

Back cover: Eagle Nebula, M16, NASA, ESA, STScI, J. Hester and P. Scowen (Arizona State University)

Anne Baring is an author and Jungian analyst. www.annebaring.com

Scilla Elworthy is the founder of Peace Direct and The Oxford Research Group. www.peacedirect.org

Made in the USA
Charleston, SC
30 December 2009

4314201